Wise Up to Rise Up:
Finding Peace and Direction in the Aftermath of Chaos

Rebecca Benston

Copyright © 2014, 2018 by Rebecca Benston (Higher Ground Books & Media)
All rights reserved. No part of this publication may be reproduced may be reproduced in any form, stored in a retrieval system, or transmitted in any form, or by any means (electronic, mechanical, photocopying, recording or otherwise) without prior permission by the copyright owner and the publisher of this book.

Unless otherwise noted, all Scripture quotations are from the Holy Bible, New International Version®, NIV® Copyright © 1973, 1978, 1984, 2011 by Biblica, Inc.®. All rights reserved worldwide.

Higher Ground Books & Media
Springfield, Ohio.
http://highergroundbooksandmedia.com

Printed in the United States of America 2018

Acknowledgements

This book is dedicated to my daughter, Mya who has been the inspiration for me to Rise Up! I love you with all my heart and I know that you will grow up to be a strong and successful woman. I pray that God blesses you all the days of your life and that you will never forget to turn to Him no matter what storms may come your way.

And I pray the same for you as you embark on this journey!

Love and Blessings,

Rebecca Benston

4

Wise Up to Rise Up:
Finding Peace and Direction in the Aftermath of Chaos

Introduction

Life is funny. Not funny in an entertaining sort of way, but funny in that we just never know when an ordinary situation is going to turn into one of the greatest challenges of our lives. After dealing with everything from alcoholism to sexual victimization it was the delivering power of Jesus Christ that brought me through and made it possible for me to have peace in my life. Looking back, I can see now where God has been with me through all of these trials; even up to the recent victimization I've suffered at the hands of a legal system that is designed to take advantage of the vulnerabilities of women.

This book is meant to be a companion guide to a workshop offered by Higher Ground Ministries called Wise Up to Rise Up. I hope you will take the opportunity to participate in this class, but if you don't, please at least work through the exercises in this book. Approach it with an open mind and answer the questions as honestly as you can. By the time you've finished the work here, you'll be able to set a new course for your life and work toward achieving all that God has designed you to achieve.

He really does make all things new and He'll wait for you. He'll be there for you long after you've given up on Him. Waiting for you to take a moment, wise up and then rise up to meet Him. So you have absolutely nothing to lose by giving Him your troubles and letting him do a work in your heart.

Wisdom, Peace & Blessings!

Rebecca Benston

PART ONE: WISE UP

CHAPTER ONE:

GETTING ON THE MAP

The most important thing you can do for yourself when you find that you are in need of transformation is to take a few moments and assess where you are currently standing. How can you move forward if you have no idea where you are? In the blanks below, write down three things you know without a doubt about where you are in your life right now. It doesn't need to be a long, complicated description. You can simply say something like, I'm a wife, I'm a mother, I'm a daughter. If that is what you know, then go with what you know. But I encourage you to dig a little deeper if you can and think about who you are really. Take five minutes or so and fill in the blanks:

I am _____

I am _____

I am _____

After completing that exercise, how do you feel about what you've written? Now, take a few minutes to think about where you would like to be. Write down three things you would like to see manifest in your life. For example, if you are single and you would like to be married, you might write something like, "I see myself in a stable, committed and loving marriage." Take five minutes and write down some things you would like to see happen in your life.

I see myself _____

I see myself _____

I see myself _____

Now, flip back and look at where you are and then compare it to where you want to be. What kind of distance lies between the two? Are you taking steps toward the things you want or standing still? Is it possible that you might even be moving in the wrong direction?

If you think you might be moving in the wrong direction, now is the time to get yourself turned around. Follow me into the next chapter and let's see what we can do to change some things.

13

CHAPTER TWO:
ENGAGING OUR NAVIGATOR

How much distance lies between where you are and where you would like to be? Often, it is hard for us to see that distance as anything but an insurmountable obstacle. But the truth is that once we can see it, we can conquer it. We cannot defeat what we don't realize is there. If we've become complacent or gotten stuck at a point in our lives where we don't have enough support to get to the next phase, it can be easy to just settle in and keep on doing what we've always done. After all, we're obviously good at it or we wouldn't still be doing it, right?

In my own experience, I've been good at many things that I probably shouldn't have been doing in the first place. And I kept on doing them because they were familiar to me. Somehow, the familiar provided a twisted kind of comfort when I was so unsure of where I needed to go and who I needed to be. But the most wonderful gift that I have ever been given is the ability now to go forward into the unknown without fear. This gift came to me through finally understanding that my relationship with God is what will give me the ability to move forward in all things.

I can do all things through Christ who strengthens me.

~Philippians 4:13 NKJV~

This idea may seem too simple for many to comprehend the depth of it, but the truth is that the effort we put forth in the flesh will net us only those rewards that the flesh can create. For years, I wore myself out trying to do things in my own effort. I tried to manipulate things to serve the purposes that I wanted them to serve in my life. All that brought was dissatisfaction, disappointment and disconnection from who I truly was and who I had wanted to become. When I finally reconnected with God, He brought me the clarity and the security that I needed to move forward and out of the destructive cycles that had done so much damage to my self-esteem.

Out of this experience, Higher Ground Ministries was born. Higher Ground Ministries is focused on helping women to become more empowered by introducing them to strategies for growth and self-improvement through living and understanding God's word and His plan for their lives. The goal of this ministry is to work on all areas of a woman's life and help her to achieve success where she may not have thought it was possible.

The first thing we need to understand as we begin to pin down where we are is the idea of a "walk" with God. This is a term used frequently to describe our relationship with Him. Christians see their journey through this life as a "walk" with God. Sometimes we're on the right path with Him; sometimes we fall off or lose our way. But as indicated in the old, favorite poem, *Footprints in the Sand*, He is always with us. During times when we think we're alone, He is not only walking with us; He's carrying us.

Where would you say you are in your walk with God at the present moment? Are you just meeting Him? Have you been "friends" for a while? Do you consider Him to be your closest confidant? Take a moment and think about what He means in your life right now. Jot down a few key words and ideas that describe where He fits into things for you.

_____

_____

_____

_____

_____

_____

_____

_____

CHAPTER THREE: SETTING OUR COURSE

The focus is on breaking down the barriers by helping to identify:

- our current position,
- our desired outcomes,
- And all of the characteristics of our current lifestyle that contribute to our ability or lack of ability to change what needs to be changed.

There will be six components that we will work through during this study. These are: self-awareness, self-esteem, self-defense, self-sufficiency, self-actualization and self-centeredness. Of these topics, which do you believe will be most challenging for you? Why?

_____

_____

_____

Each of these will be broken down into lessons that include Scriptural references to help us to begin to develop a solid foundation in Christ. These lessons will also include recommended readings to help you learn more about each topic. We will eventually be able to use what we have learned to help other women learn and they will be able to do the same. So…let's begin!

CHAPTER FOUR: SELF-AWARENESS

What good is it for someone to gain the whole world, and yet lose or forfeit their very self?

~Luke 9:25~

Learn to be aware of those traits which we possess that can either help or hinder our progress.

What we deny or what we fail to acknowledge will eventually surface and keep us from achieving our goals. Confront your weaknesses; Satan knows what our fears are. Well-known author and Bible teacher, Beth Moore says that he is counting on the fact that he can convince us of our worst fears about ourselves. Why? Because we're often in denial or simply not paying attention. Be honest with yourself about the person you are and the person you have been. Don't let guilt consume you if you've done wrong in your life; just understand what was wrong with it and why it had to happen in your life. Is there something you feel guilty over that you can't seem to let go? Complete the sentence below:

Today, I will let go of my guilt over

_____.

No matter what it is, no matter when it happened, you must absolutely forgive yourself for the things you feel you have messed up in your life in order to be able to move forward. God will forgive you and if you have accepted Him as your Savior, He has already forgiven you. There is no need to stay under condemnation. You have been made new!

__Therefore, if anyone is in Christ, he is a new creation; old things have passed away; behold, all things have become new.__

~2 Corinthians 5:17 NKJV~

Some helpful Scripture for self-awareness can be found here:

2 Corinthians 13:5 ESV

Examine yourselves, to see whether you are in the faith. Test yourselves. Or do you not realize this about yourselves, that Jesus Christ is in you?—unless indeed you fail to meet the test!

2 Peter 1:3 ESV

His divine power has granted to us all things that pertain to life and godliness, through the knowledge of him who called us to his own glory and excellence,

Proverbs 14:8 ESV

The wisdom of the prudent is to discern his way, but the folly of fools is deceiving.

CHAPTER FIVE:

SELF-ESTEEM

Rather, it should be that of your inner self, the unfading beauty of a gentle and quiet spirit, which is of great worth in God's sight.

~1 Peter 3:4~

Our attitude toward ourselves. Do we like ourselves? Do we respect ourselves?

Depending upon the tapes that are playing in our heads, we can feel either motivated or condemned. If you grew up in an environment where people were critical of you or abusive, the messages that you hear on a continuous loop may not be the kinds of messages that will spur you on toward victory. It's time to replace those messages with the truth of God's word. You are more than worthy as God's creation and He wants you to know your worth. Repeat the following statement to yourself daily as an affirmation that you are God's beloved child:

I am His child and He lives in me.

You are His masterpiece and He has a Divine purpose for your life. He sent His only Son to die for the sins of all mankind and that includes you. There is nothing you can do to keep Him from loving you. He lives in you.

Some helpful Scripture for rebuilding our self-esteem can be found in:

Genesis 1:27NKJV

So God created man in His own image; in the image of God He created him; male and female He created them.

Job 33:4 NKJV

The Spirit of God has made me, and the breath of the Almighty gives me life.

Psalm 8:3-5 NKJV

When I look at your heavens, the work of your fingers, the moon and the stars, which you have set in place, What is man that You are mindful of him, And the son of man that You visit him? For You have made him a little lower than the angels, And You have crowned him with glory and honor.

Psalm 139:13-15 NKJV

For You formed my inward parts; You covered me in my mother's womb I will praise You, for I am fearfully and wonderfully made; Marvelous are Your works, And that my soul knows very well. My frame was not hidden from You, when I was made in secret, And skillfully wrought in the lowest parts of the earth.

CHAPTER SIX:

SELF-DEFENSE

Therefore put on the full armor of God, so that when the day of evil comes, you may be able to stand your ground, and after you have done everything, to stand.

~Ephesians 6:13~

Being able to identify and protect yourself against emotional, physical and psychological threats.

This one can be tough. Sometimes even when we follow what we think is right, everything blows up in our faces. The key is to take time to slow down and spend some time talking with God and reviewing His word to see what lines up. What resonates in your Spirit as the right thing? Sometimes we may put ourselves on auto-pilot and simply move forward because we see no immediate threat. The threat, however; can lay a little further down the road and trip us up when we are just starting to feel safe. This isn't always the case, but we must always make time to ask God for discernment if we wish to make solid decisions. If not, we must prepare ourselves to accept the consequences of our decisions, knowing that whatever happens is part of God's plan for us. He is never surprised by our choices and if we are truly trying to walk in relationship with Him, He will not let us fall.

One of the biggest games the enemy will play is to try and keep us in a state of fear. God does not want us to be afraid. He has given us everything we need to fight off these attacks; we just need to figure out how to access that "armor." One thing that can be helpful here is to try and pinpoint the kinds of things we are already using as our personal defense mechanisms. What have you been using as your "armor"? Take a moment and jot down a few of you own personal defense mechanisms.

_____

_____

_____

_____

_____

_____

_____

_____

_____

Some helpful Scriptures for guarding our hearts can be found here:

Deuteronomy 23:14 NIV

For the Lord your God moves about in your camp to protect you and to deliver your enemies to you. Your camp must be holy, so that he will not see among you anything indecent and turn away from you.

Psalm 20:1 NIV

May the Lord answer you when you are in distress; may the name of the God of Jacob protect you.

Psalm 32:7 NIV

You are my hiding place; you will protect me from trouble and surround me with songs of deliverance.

2 Thessalonians 3:3 NIV

But the Lord is faithful, and he will strengthen you and protect you from the evil one.

CHAPTER SEVEN:

SELF-SUFFICIENCY

Have I not commanded you? Be strong and courageous. Do not be afraid; do not be discouraged, for the Lord your God will be with you wherever you go."

~Joshua 1:9~

The ability to take care of one's own physical, emotional, psychological, and spiritual needs.

Throughout life there may be times when we are unable to support ourselves in the manner we would like. This can wear on our resolve and make us feel as though we aren't good enough. The truth is that we are never really completely self-sufficient. The good news is that the One on whom we can rely will always provide exactly what we need when we need it.

Our understanding of this concept is the key to keeping our hopes up in times of trouble. But, even more important than this realization is the understanding that when we think we need it may not be when He sees that we need it. His timing is perfect and He will not allow us to suffer when we put our faith and trust in Him. We must understand that trusting Him means that even when it looks like He isn't going to come through, we can still depend on His faithfulness. And we can be assured that when we receive our blessing that will be the exact time that He means it to show up.

Are there areas in your life where you are waiting for provision? List them here and in your prayer time, remember to acknowledge that He will provide at the appointed time.

Lord, you know my need(s) and I trust in Your timing and Your provision.

_____

_____

_____

_____

_____

Some verses that might help you apply this concept:

Matthew 6:8 NIV

Do not be like them, for your Father knows what you need before you ask him.

2 Corinthians 9:8 NIV

And God is able to bless you abundantly, so that in all things at all times, having all that you need, you will abound in every good work.

1 Timothy 5:5

The widow who is really in need and left all alone puts her hope in God and continues night and day to pray and to ask God for help.

CHAPTER EIGHT:

SELF-ACTUALIZATION

In everything he did he had great success,

because the LORD was with him.

~1 Samuel 18:14~

Reaching our ultimate fulfillment.

Coming to a place where we are able to achieve the goals we set for ourselves happens when we align our goals with the plan the God has set for us. We can blindly move toward our goals and achieve milestone after milestone without having our eyes on God, but those achievements will never provide the fulfillment that achieving a God-centered goal provides. The point of working toward fulfillment is to reflect God's glory through what we achieve. If our actions are only bringing attention and glory to us, then they are not rooted deeply enough to be of any lasting value.

So how do we center our life goals on a plan that God hasn't yet revealed to us? Good question. We first have to be completely honest with ourselves about what we know He has given us. What talents do you have? What comes easily to you? Where do you find your greatest satisfaction? He has revealed to you more than you realize. Write down three things you believe that God has shown you about yourself?

_____

_____

_____

_____

_____

How do these things connect to the goals you have set for yourself?

_____

_____

_____

_____

Can you see a connection between the gifts He has given you and the goals you believed you had set for yourself? (Write a brief summary)

_____

_____

_____

Some Scripture that might be helpful with this concept:

Proverbs 16:9 NIV

In their hearts humans plan their course, but the Lord establishes their steps.

Proverbs 21:30 NIV

There is no wisdom, no insight, no plan that can succeed against the Lord.

Ephesians 1:11 NIV

In him we were also chosen, having been predestined according to the plan of him who works out everything in conformity with the purpose of his will,

CHAPTER NINE:

SELF-CENTEREDNESS

If you carefully observe all these commands I am giving you to follow—to love the LORD your God, to walk in obedience to him and to hold fast to him—

~Deuteronomy 11:22~

More appropriately, God-centeredness. To love ourselves as a result of our understanding of God's undying, unconditional love for us.

When we hear the term "self-centered," it often conjures up images of those who are so wrapped up in their own lives that they can't seem to see anything but their own needs. The kind of self-centeredness I'm talking about here, however; is a true understanding of who we are at our core and how God lives in us.

When we begin to walk in obedience to God's word, He comes to dwell in us. And we are no longer just us; we are the righteousness of Christ. And so, being centered on the Great I Am, we can know that we are doing what is right and good by keeping the focus on God and how His glory is to be magnified in our actions.

How do your actions reflect the goodness of God? This is your time to brag a little on yourself…because you are, of course, giving praise to the One whose glory is in you. Share a few things here.

_____

_____

_____

_____

Are there areas where there is too much you and not enough Him shining through? Discuss.

_____

_____

_____

_____

As we talked about in the last chapter, there is a connection between the good we perceive ourselves doing and how God's glory is manifesting in our actions even when we don't see it. Take a look at what you've written above. Can you see the connections now that they are written down in front of you?

_____

_____

_____

_____

Here are some verses to help you live this out:

1 John 3:24 NLT

Those who obey God's commandments remain in fellowship with him, and he with them. And we know he lives in us because the Spirit he gave us lives in us.

1 John 4:12 NLT

No one has ever seen God. But if we love each other, God lives in us, and his love is brought to full expression in us.

Romans 5:2 NLT

Because of our faith, Christ has brought us into this place of undeserved privilege where we now stand, and we confidently and joyfully look forward to sharing God's glory.

2 Corinthians 4:7 NIV

We now have this light shining in our hearts, but we ourselves are like fragile clay jars containing this great treasure. This makes it clear that our great power is from God, not from ourselves.

PART TWO: RISE UP

CHAPTER TEN:

WHERE ARE YOU NOW?

Then the Lord God called to the man,

"Where are you?"

~Genesis 3:9 NIV~

In order to gain ground, you must first assess where you currently stand. To do this, we will go through three steps over the next few chapters:

- *Map Exercise*
- *"Dream Coordinates"*
- *History and Position*

The First Step: Map Exercise

If you were drawing a map, how would you represent your current position? When I first began trying to assess where I was, my map looked something like this:

Family/Faith Priority

The sections of the heart represent how much of my heart belongs to each of these aspects of my life. On the left is family, on the right is faith and at the bottom is work. You'll notice that the portion of my heart that is dedicated to work is quite small. This does not mean that I'm lazy. It just means that I value my family and faith more than the work I do. It wasn't always this way.

At one point in my life, I was highly ambitious and as I look back on it, I believe I took my work way too seriously. God was not at the center of my life. He wasn't even on the radar. A bi-product of this was a lack of focus on my family. I wasn't a bad mother or wife, but I wasn't the best I could be. But when I returned to Him after years of thinking the worst about Christians, work took a backseat to faith and family became more of a priority as a result of my new-found faith. Now, if I'm forced to sacrifice either family or faith to continue working, I will opt to find different work because God has shown me new priorities and He has shown me time and time again that He will provide.

Here's how this shift in consciousness began:

Shortly after I had made the decision to fully dedicate myself to the Lord, my marriage finally finished falling apart. I moved out of the house with my daughter and I took on a new position with the company where I had been working. The new position required me to move to a new building and to work with a new supervisor. In my previous position, I had been permitted to express my faith freely; in fact, the culture in the building where I worked was actually very pro-Christian. In my new building, the atmosphere shifted and I found that any mention of my faith was basically forbidden. Same organization, same company policies, different building philosophy.

One day, I had sent an e-mail out to my co-workers to let them know of an upcoming fundraising event that was being held in another of our buildings. The fundraiser would benefit a program that had been in place in our organization for years. The same day I sent the e-mail, my supervisor came to tell me that I needed to remove my personalized footer from my e-mail because someone found it offensive.

My footer, which had been on my e-mail for the past three years, was a Bible verse. It read,

> *"But blessed are those who trust in the Lord*
> *and have made the Lord their hope and confidence.*
> *They are like trees planted along a riverbank,*
> *with roots that reach deep into the water.*
> *Such trees are not bothered by the heat*
> *or worried by long months of drought.*
> *Their leaves stay green,*
> *and they never stop producing fruit."*
>
> **Jeremiah 17:7-8 *(New Living Translation)***

Suddenly, this Bible verse was offensive to someone. Never mind that my supervisors and higher ups in the administration had all received e-mails from me for the past three years and no one had a problem with it until I was working for this particular individual. This ended up being the first true test of my faith that I realized I was facing. Of course, there had been other tests, but it wasn't until this point in my life that I understood the meaning of religious discrimination.

After several weeks of going back and forth and being threatened with termination, I finally took the verse off of my footer. I was under contract at the time and decided that I would finish out my time with the organization and then take my leave. Over the course of that year, I was reprimanded seven times for minor infractions. These were clearly the result of my having attempted to stand my ground after the e-mail incident. There was really nothing I could do, so I just finished out my term and then resigned.

At the time, I was terrified. What in the world would I do for work? How would I support my daughter and myself? It was yet another test of my faith, but as usual, the Lord came through. Within weeks, I had some freelance writing to do and I was able to find ways to make ends meet. The next few years would prove treacherous on the work front, but never once did my cupboards go bare and never once was I without shelter and clothing and everything that we needed to survive. The point I'm trying to make here is that when we are able to pinpoint the areas of our lives where we focus our energies, we'll have a much easier time figuring out whether or not we're on the right path. But we first have to identify what path, if any, we are on. Looking at the examples below, which would you say best describes your location on the map:

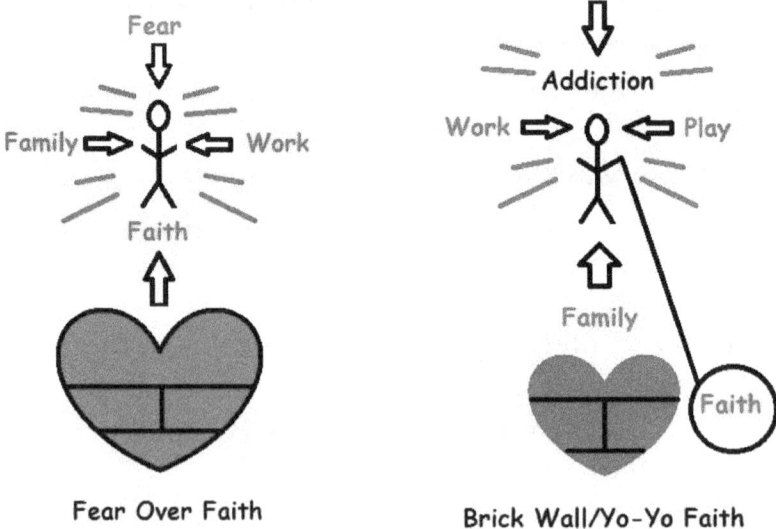

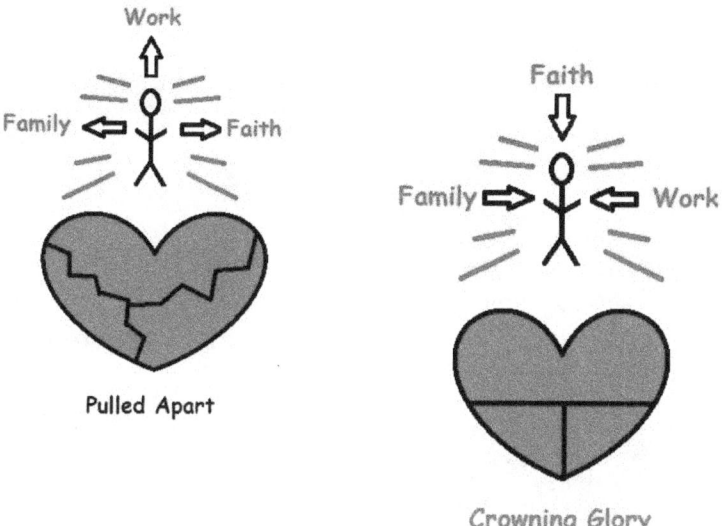

There are many examples and each one is unique to the heart that contains it. The idea here is to get you thinking about what your heart looks like now and where this puts you on the roadmap of your life.

To further explain the examples given:

The Fear Over Faith model occurs when fear occupies more of your heart than anything else. The heart diagram shows that family and work are split down the middle and there is just a little room for faith at the bottom. All of these contribute to a lack of focus on God's plan for us, even though we are at least allowing a little bit of faith to creep into our consciousness.

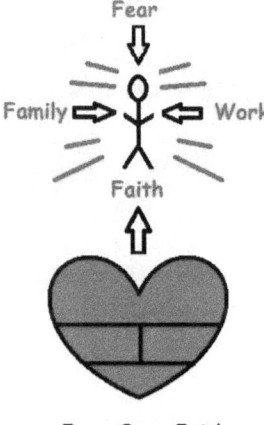

Fear Over Faith

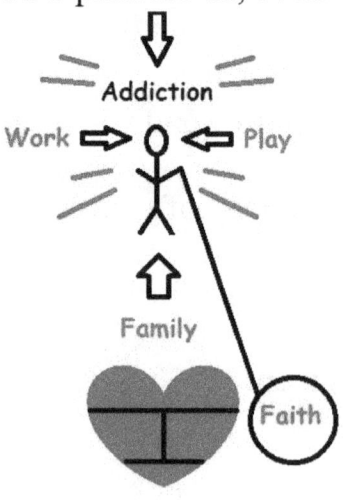

Brick Wall/Yo-Yo Faith

The Brick Wall/Yo-Yo Faith model is typical of many of us, although we may not realize that we are living this way. Some addictions are full-blown, but others are trickier to identify. What happens here is that we are living our lives with a focus on fitting everything in that we want to do and we hold our faith on a string, reeling it in when we need it and letting it down when things are going okay. The addiction could be food, alcohol, drugs, sex, gambling, social networking, video games, porn, or anything that becomes a permanent fixture that we work to maintain and center our play around. Family, of course, takes a backseat to all of it because it just happens to be something we have to deal with.

The Pulled Apart model is somewhat self-explanatory.

Pulled Apart

As you can see from the diagram, we are pulled in different directions by a combination of work, family and faith. The end result is that our heart suffers brokenness and none of what we are doing is effective.

Crowning Glory

Ideally, our hearts would look like this model:

The Crowning Glory model shows the largest portion of the heart dedicated to faith with a healthy balance between family and work. No addictions, no fixations, no brokenness. This may seem almost impossible to achieve, but as it says in Matthew 19:26 NLT, with God all things are possible.

Some verses about the heart:

1 Kings 8:39 NLT

…then hear from heaven where you live, and forgive. Give your people what their actions deserve, for you alone know each human heart.

2 Chronicles 19:9 NLT

These were his instructions to them: "You must always act in the fear of the Lord, with faithfulness and an undivided heart.

Psalm 16:7 NLT

I will bless the Lord who guides me; even at night my heart instructs me.

Psalm 40:8 NLT

I take joy in doing your will, my God, for your instructions are written on my heart.

Romans 15:32 NLT

Then, by the will of God, I will be able to come to you with a joyful heart, and we will be an encouragement to each other.

69

CHAPTER ELEVEN:

WHERE WOULD YOU LIKE TO BE?

"Listen to this dream," he said.

~Genesis 37:6 NLT~

The Second Step: "Dream Coordinates"

When we think about goal setting, the big question is always, "Where do you want to be?" For our purposes here though, we aren't going to do any goal setting just yet. We are going to look at the work we've just done in the last chapter and then think in terms of how our whole life has led up to this point. We must understand this before we go any further.

Look at the entire picture from start to present and include all aspects of your life. This means financial, spiritual, physical, emotional, mental and anything else that has impacted you. Now let's connect some dots. What brought you happiness? What brought you grief? What were your reactions to these things?

Now that you look at things from a total picture perspective, can you see where certain decisions might have led you in the right direction? Or led you astray? From here, you can begin looking forward. It's not an instantaneous thing, but once you have seen how it all fits together up to your current position in life you are at a much better vantage point to begin setting future goals. And if you haven't already, you can now begin setting them with God's path for you in mind. Now, think big and GO FOR IT!!!!!

With all of this in mind, list three new goals below:

_____

_____

_____

Now, looking at your newly formed goals, take a few minutes to think about where you are and where you want to be. What is the distance between the two? These questions may help you with that answer:

- Where are you now…ex. In debt. Unhappy with my job.
- Where would you like to be?...ex. Debt-free. In a career that fits me and provides for my financial freedom.
- What is the actual distance between the two?...ex. More education, More money, Better job, Better relationships.

Some verses to help you with this concept:

Job 36:25 NLT

Everyone has seen these things, though only from a distance.

Genesis 27:20 NLT

Isaac asked, "How did you find it so quickly, my son?" "The Lord your God put it in my path!" Jacob replied.

Psalm 18:36 NLT

You have made a wide path for my feet to keep them from slipping.

Psalm 25:4 NLT

Show me the right path, O Lord; point out the road for me to follow.

CHAPTER TWELVE:

WHERE DID YOU COME FROM?

Let me share in the prosperity of your chosen ones. Let me rejoice in the joy of your people; let me praise you with those who are your heritage.

~ *Psalm 106:5 NLT*~

In order to know where we are going, we must first know and acknowledge where we've been. Things in our past which did not make sense at the time may well make perfect sense a few years after the fact. In my experience, it took years for me to gain enough clarity and emotional distance from the traumas I suffered to be able to make any sense out of them. And while I couldn't always make perfect sense of what had happened, I could see the purpose behind why it did and how that experience had prepared me for a new phase in my life.

My childhood taught me lessons that have been very valuable in surviving some of the things I've encountered as an adult. Being a rape survivor game me special insight into how to help women who have, themselves, been victims. Having five miscarriages helped to prepare me for other losses that would occur later. And all of these things forced me to have faith that there was some purpose that I couldn't yet see.

How has your past influenced your vision of the future? When I was going through years of pain after having been victimized by someone whom I had thought was a friend, my vision of the future was cut off. The only hopes I had at that point were of getting through the current day and somehow waking up the next morning without being hurt again. It was a terrifying time and one during which I was not walking with God. Yet, He still had a hand on me. He still reached down into that pit and brought me to higher ground. Little by little, he put the pieces back together. He brought me through a bout of alcoholism, sex addiction, and a self-destructive cycle that I'm now certain was a product of the devil's immense hatred of God's unfailing love for me.

    I did not gain a vision for the future until I was feeling safe again. God provided that safety for me even when I wasn't willing to acknowledge that He was the one providing it. He knew that I would find my way back to Him eventually and He never let me go. And even though for a time, I felt stuck, things eventually happened to break me out of the cycle of self-destruction and I was able to begin building upward…with God's help, of course. I messed up from time to time; everyone does. But I was not so in love with the past that had held me hostage for so long that I couldn't see the wonderful blessings that lay ahead on the path God had set for me. Think about your past and some of the things that might be clouding your vision. Are you stuck? Are you still hanging onto things that you need to let go of?

Take a moment and jot down your thoughts on this chapter. Answer some of the questions posed above:

_____

_____

CHAPTER THIRTEEN: HOW FAR DO YOU HAVE LEFT TO GO?

Then they said to him, "Please inquire of God to learn whether our journey will be successful."

~ Judges 18:5 NIV~

Sometimes we can get so caught up in planning the journey and engaging in the struggles that accompany it that we forget why we started heading in that direction to begin with. We must take time to assess where we are and where we intend to go in order to ensure that the whole thing still makes sense for us. You may find that where you once intended to go no longer makes sense for you because you've changed along the way. Ask yourself whether or not it still makes sense to pursue that goal and if it does, then you can determine how much progress you've made and how far you still need to go before you've achieved success.

    Take a look at your current situation. In the picture on the following page, the person is looking in the direction of her goals and envisioning that the path will be clear. Take a look at your dreams. Can you remember what they are? Did you ever

really know?

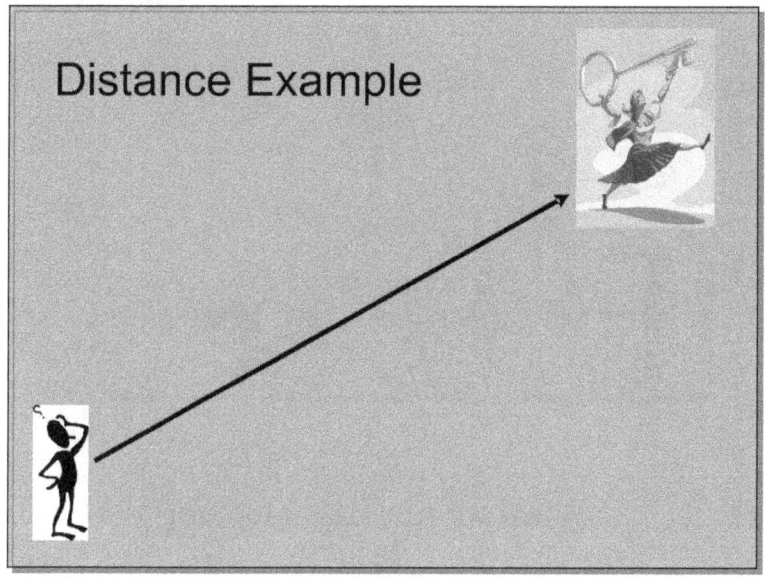

We all know that no journey ever runs

this smoothly. In fact, they generally look

more like this:

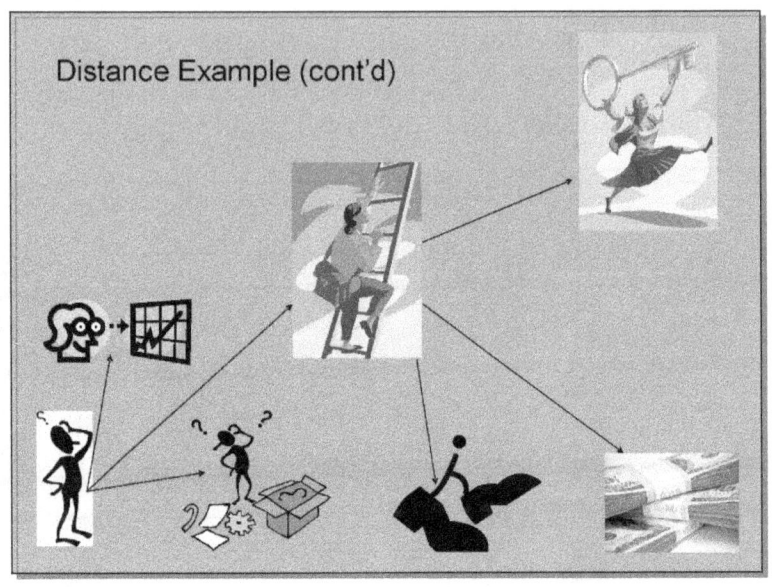

When we first begin looking at where we are, we often can easily see the dream and the many pieces of it that will undoubtedly confuse us. Just beyond that, we can maybe even see ourselves climbing toward success. But sometimes this vision obscures the vision of our actually reaching that success. In addition, we often get sidetracked by feeling that those "shoes are too big to fill" or that we might not have the resources to reach our goals.

If we work really hard at achieving our goals, we are bound to encounter problems at every turn. It is a well-known fact that whenever we make progress toward advancing God's kingdom purposes for our lives, the devil is bound to throw obstacles in our path. That's why our journeys often appear to be so disjointed. But it's all meant to work together for our good and God always knows the outcome of each and every decision that we make. He is never surprised by what we do.

In truth, once we achieve a goal, there will always be another one just beyond it. And beyond that, another. If we are living this life to serve God and His purpose for us, we will not be finished until the day He takes us home. If we are focused on hearing His voice and following His path for us, it helps the journey to look a bit more like this:

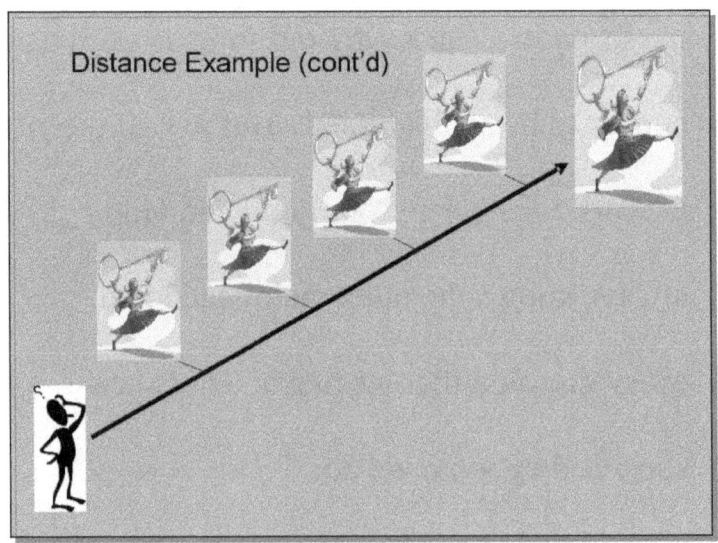

CHAPTER FOURTEEN:

FINISHING YOUR RACE

I have fought the good fight, I have finished the race, I have kept the faith.

~ 2 Timothy 4:7 NIV~

There are many ways to get past the obstacles we face in life. The point of the journey is that we would bring glory to God through overcoming the struggles we encounter. He has planned out our lives and He knows where He wants us to be at every point along the way. Look back at your successes and your failures and reframe them in light of what you've learned through these lessons.

List out at least three transitions that you've gone through in your life:

1. _____

_____

2. _____

_____

3. _____

_____

List three things you consider to be successes:

1. _____

_____

2. _____

_____

3. _____

_____

Now list three things that you consider to be failures:

1. _____

_____

2. _____

_____

3. _____

_____

Why do you see the last three as failures?

_____

_____

_____

Can you see the value in those experiences looking at them from this side of things?

_____

_____

_____

_____

_____

_____

CHAPTER FIFTEEN:

CONCLUSION

Rise up; this matter is in your hands. We will support you, so take courage and do it."

~ Ezra 10:4 NIV~

Even if you can't see it now, eventually you will look back on experiences which once confused you and caused you pain and you'll be able to understand the meaning and significance of those things as they relate to your current situation. God reveals things to us in His time, not ours. But in order to understand His plan, we must seek to understand His word and the lessons that have already been learned by so many who came before us. By the examples set forth in the teachings of the Bible we can see the significance of facing our challenges and replacing our fear with faith in an Almighty God.

You can overcome the challenges that life has thrown you. The willingness to change is the first step toward restoration. Knowing our weaknesses can reveal the great strengths that lie inside us. The journey is an ongoing process, but we can't move forward until we acknowledge that it is time for a change.

So get moving! It's time to Rise Up!

Other titles from Higher Ground Books & Media:

A Path to Shalom by Steen Burke
From a Hole in My Life to a Life Made Whole by Janet Kay Teresa
Overcomer by Forrest Henslee
Miracles: I Love Them by Forest Godin
32 Days with Christ's Passion by Mark Etter
The Magic Egg by Linda Phillipson
The Tin Can Gang by Chuck David
Whobert the Owl by Mya C. Benston
Out of Darkness by Stephen Bowman
Knowing Affliction and Doing Recovery by John Baldasare
A Practical Guide to Better Behaved Children by John Salmon, PhD
Love's Resurrection by Daniel K. Held
I Don't Want to Be Like You by Maryanne Christiano-Mistretta
Add these titles to your collection today!
http://highergroundbooksandmedia.com

www.ingramcontent.com/pod-product-compliance
Lightning Source LLC
Chambersburg PA
CBHW020016050426
42450CB00005B/499